The Sad Skeleton

by Kay Brophy

with illustrations by Katy Boys

First published in the UK in 2016 by Middle Farm Press
British Library Cataloguing-in-Publication Data
A catalogue record for this book is available from the British Library
ISBN 978-0-9928896-3-0
This edition 2017
2 3 4 5 6 7 8 9 10

Published by Middle Farm Press
Author: Kay Brophy
Managing Editor: Kate Taylor
Illustrator: Katy Boys
Designer: Su Richards
Printed by Think Digital Books Ltd

Acorn

MIDDLE FARM PRESS

To my kids, Niamh and Dan

Lifeland
Station
STATION OF SURPRISE
ANGER ARCHES
SAD STONES

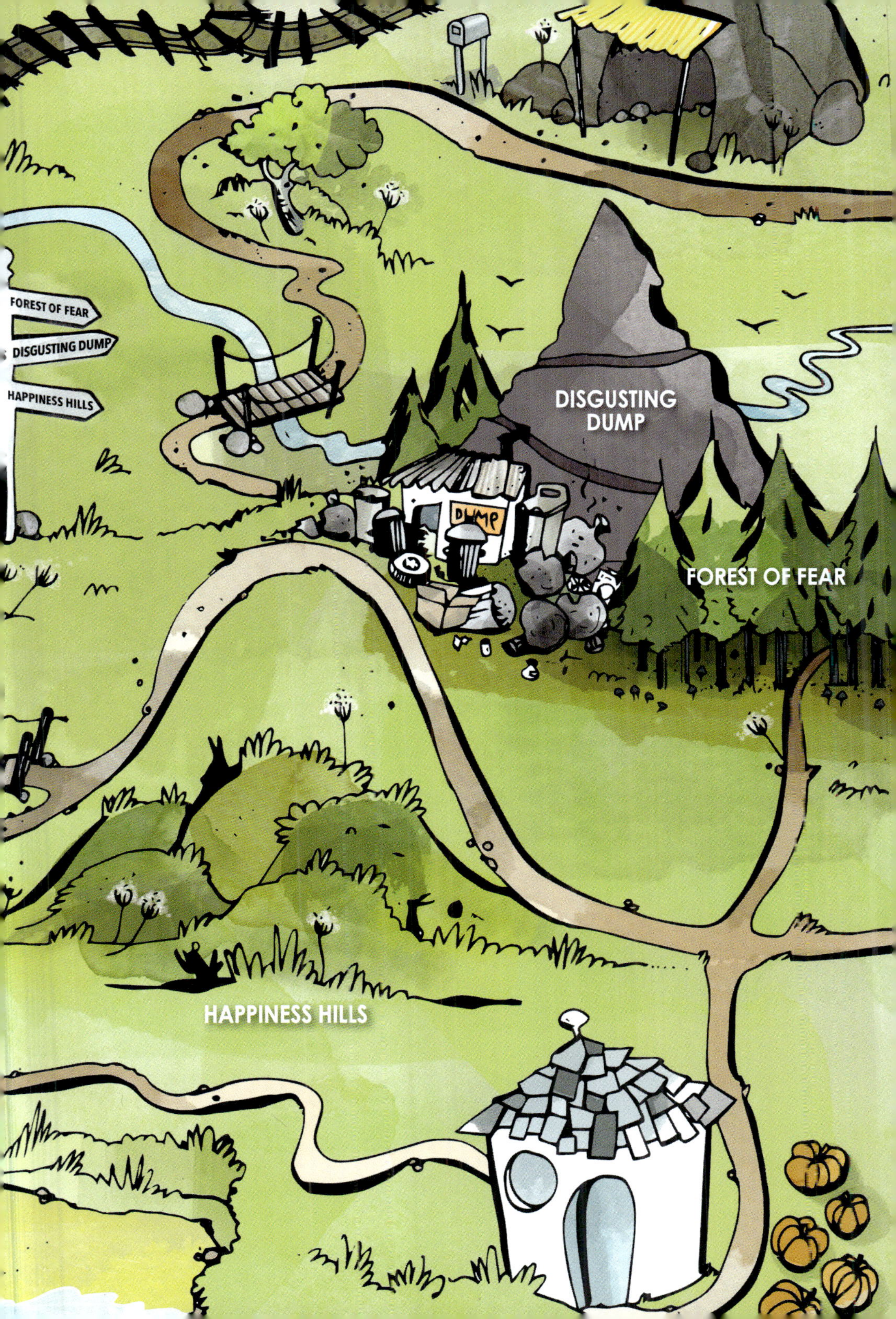
FOREST OF FEAR
DISGUSTING DUMP
HAPPINESS HILLS
DISGUSTING
DUMP
DUMP
FOREST OF FEAR
HAPPINESS HILLS

There once was a Skeleton
kind as could be
But people would stare
and then instantly flee

The truth was this Skeleton

was lonely and sad

He didn't like to be thought of

as bony and bad

'I don't like looking scary,
It's not really me'
'I'd rather dress up and wear
fun things you see'

'A teddy bear onesie would
be perfect right now'
'I'm sure it would help
this reaction somehow'

So Skeleton was sad but nobody knew
He thought and he thought... what could he do?
He needed some help and he needed it fast
It was time to leave Lostland and find a new path

Skeleton was friends
with a black bat called Dave
He was smart and funny
and lived in a cave

'I'll pay Dave a visit'
the Skeleton said
'I'll ask why these 'thoughts' are
hurting my head'

TO SWIM WITH WINGS
Sustainable Moth hunting
THE BIG BUG COOK BOOK
CAVES of THE WORLD
HOW TO FLY WITHOUT GETTING IN A FLAP
SUNBATHING INDOORS
Two Bats
B
HOVER fly ISCUITS
organic MOTHS

'The problem is simple' Dave finally replied
'You are different from others on the outside'

'You are bony and skinless and terribly tall'
'To others you probably look frightening, that's all'

'Oh' said the Skeleton 'I hear what you say'
'So the way that I look scares the people away?'

'Skeletons ALWAYS look scary and mean'
'At least they are in the books
and films that I've seen'

Then all of a sudden

he didn't know why

The confused Sad Skeleton

started to cry

It moved through his body and he started to shake
His bones made a rattle and continued to quake

Dave hung quite still and
listened with care
He knew that his friend
did not want to scare

The talking made Skeleton feel
calmer and brave
He had shared all his fears
and his worries with Dave

Suddenly he said 'I have an idea'
'I think I can help them get over
their fear'

'I just need some shades
and a pair of headphones'
'And a long cape and trousers
to cover my bones'

In just a few hours the
costume was done
'Now let's go out and have
us some fun'

He walked through the land, and mile after mile
He heard none of them scream but saw all of them smile

The Skeleton discovered something
important that day
He found that 'big' feelings CAN go away

After all the excitement,
Skeleton headed to bed
In his teddy bear onesie
he rested his head
His friend had been there
to help him get through
And if you're ever sad,
he will be there for you

USER GUIDE FOR TEACHERS, PARENTS AND CARERS

All children, in every walk of life, will struggle with their feelings from time to time. The Sad Skeleton is part of a series of books called Finding Your Way. Each book takes one of the six 'big' feelings of sadness, fear, anger, happiness, surprise and disgust and shows the reader how to explore, identify and manage the feeling safely on their own or with the help of an adult.

HOW TO USE THIS BOOK

This book can be read with a child or a group of children at any time, and will be particularly useful if the child is, or has been, experiencing sad feelings. Rather than focusing on the child themselves, the adult should focus on the character's feelings. For example, talking about how the Skeleton is feeling will help the child to feel safe. Adults can use the pictures within the book to aid them.

USING THE FIVE Ws

Example questions you could ask while reading this book:

- **W**hy do you think the Skeleton is sad?
- **W**hat do you think he should do?
- **W**here is he in Lifeland?
- **W**ho can help him with his feelings?
- **W**hen does the Skeleton feel happy?

Sometimes when children are sad they may also be experiencing other feelings such as fear, anger, surprise or disgust. Adults can help the child explore these feelings using the Lifeland map at the front of the book. As you read through the book together try to encourage the child to think about where the Skeleton is on the map. For example, when he is in Dave's cave you could show the child where the cave is located on the map, exploring feelings and places together.

DID YOU KNOW?

- Reading with your child at least four times a week can help them to develop their own reading and literacy skills.
- Talking to your child about feelings can help them develop their emotional language and intelligence.